TABLE OF CONTENTS

IN DEPTH: DRIP STYLEZ & CUTZ

DRIP STYLEZ & CUTZ: WHERE HISTORY MEETS HAIR MASTERY IN CHICAGO'S BRONZEVILLE DISTRICT

At 'Drip Stylez & Cutz,' the art of barbering is elevated to a level of excellence. The skilled hands of the master barber craft haircuts that are nothing short of masterpieces. From classic gentleman's cuts to trendy fades and intricate designs, each stroke of the blade and snip of the scissors is executed with precision and a deep understanding of the client's unique style.

Beyond its mastery of barbering, 'Drip Stylez & Cutz' plays a vital role in the Bronzeville community. It's a place where neighbors become friends, where stories are shared, and where bonds are forged. The barbershop is not just a place to get a haircut; it's a hub of culture, history, and camaraderie.

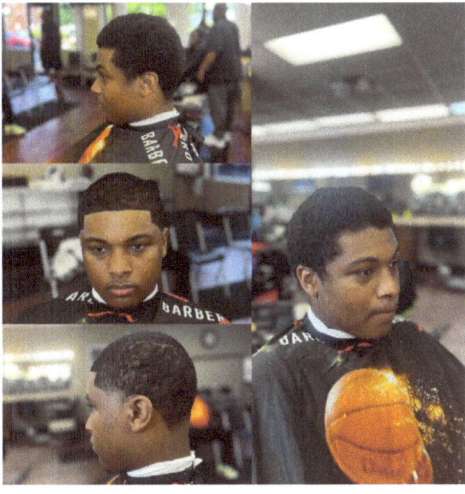
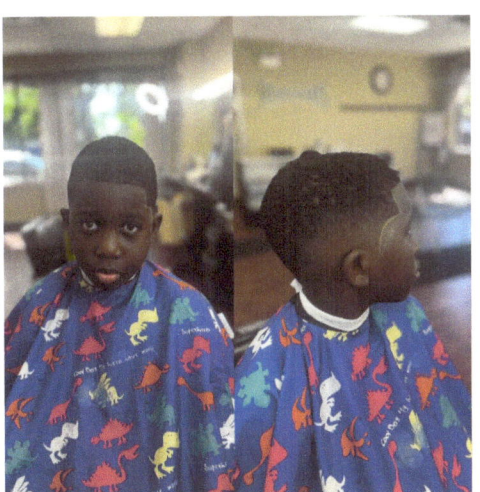

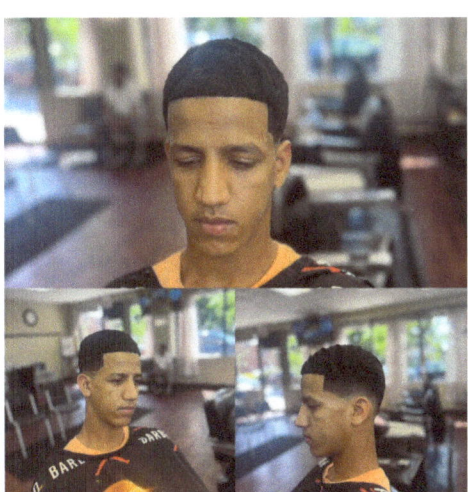

Drip Stylez & Cutz' takes pride in its aesthetic appeal as well. The shop's interior is a fusion of modern design and vintage charm, paying homage to the rich history of Bronzeville. Every detail, from the comfortable waiting area to the meticulous attention given to cleanliness and hygiene, reflects the commitment to excellence that defines this establishment.

Bronzeville has a storied past, and 'Drip Stylez & Cutz' stands as a contemporary crown jewel in this historical district. It's a place where the old meets the new, where tradition blends seamlessly with innovation. For those who appreciate the art of barbering and the spirit of community, 'Drip Stylez & Cutz' is not just a barbershop; it's an embodiment of Bronzeville's enduring legacy and a beacon of excellence in the heart of Chicago.

ELEVATING CHICAGO'S STYLE SCENE, ONE CHIC WARDROBE AT A TIME

Nestled in the heart of Chicago's bustling fashion district, Leighas Lane Collection stands as a beacon of timeless elegance and sartorial innovation. This chic boutique, with its warm and inviting ambiance, offers fashion enthusiasts a unique shopping experience unlike any other. The brainchild of visionary designer Leigha, Leighas Lane Collection has redefined the fashion landscape in the Windy City, becoming a coveted destination for those seeking a perfect blend of style, sophistication, and individuality.

Leighas Lane Collection boasts a stunning array of dresses and rompers that embody the essence of effortless elegance. From flowing maxi dresses perfect for a night out on the town to cute rompers ideal for summer adventures, you'll find a diverse collection that suits any occasion. Each piece is carefully designed to enhance your unique style and elevate your fashion game, making every day an opportunity to express yourself.

LEIGHAS LANE

4

For those yearning for sun-soaked escapes, Leighas Lane Collection offers a delightful range of bikinis and beachwear that will make you stand out by the shore. Whether you're basking in the sun on Lake Michigan or exploring exotic beaches afar, you'll discover swimsuits that combine fashion-forward design with comfortable wear, ensuring you look and feel your best in every seaside moment.

The boutique's collection of two-piece sets epitomizes versatility and trendiness. Whether you're looking for a casual-cool ensemble for brunch with friends or a sophisticated look for a special event, Leghas Lane Collection has you covered. These sets are designed to effortlessly transition from day to night, offering you the flexibility to adapt to any social setting.

Leighas Lane Collection embodies the spirit of Chicago's fashion-forward urban scene while catering to the diverse tastes and lifestyles of its clientele. With its unwavering commitment to quality and style, this boutique has become a fashion mecca where you can explore, experiment, and discover the perfect pieces to express your unique identity. Step into Leghas Lane Collection and embark on a fashion journey that promises to elevate your style quotient, one stunning piece at a time.

DR. DOLL'S
THE PERSUITE BOUTIQUE

Dr. Doll: Transforming Lives with "The PerSUITE Boutique" - A Virtual Oasis of Healing and Learning

Dr. Doll emerges as a remarkable character in the ever-changing environment of healthcare and education, pioneering a comprehensive approach to healing trauma and unfavorable childhood experiences. "The PerSUITE Boutique," Dr. Doll's innovative endeavor, elegantly merges her duties as a compassionate therapist and an educator, providing a virtual haven where individuals can explore the complexity of trauma and poor childcare experiences. She is illuminating a route to understanding, healing, and empowerment through her online practice and courses.

"The PerSUITE Boutique" is more than just a website; it's a space of information, healing, and transformation. Dr. Doll's courses offer a complete road map for those who want to understand and heal from traumatic circumstances, building resilience and growth. The platform demonstrates her steadfast dedication to assisting individuals who have faced life's most difficult challenges. Dr. Doll's work exemplifies the limitless potential of internet platforms to impact positive, long-term change in the lives of those seeking peace and regeneration.

Dr. Doll's commitment extends beyond the usual confines of her profession, as she constantly pushes the envelope to redefine what is possible in the worlds of virtual healthcare and education. Through "The PerSUITE Boutique," she is providing a lifeline to countless people seeking mental well-being. Dr. Doll is a guiding light for those seeking insight, healing, and personal transformation in the midst of life's most difficult problems, with an unparalleled blend of compassion, expertise, and inventiveness. Her virtual practice and educational activities demonstrate the tremendous potential of digital environments to support profound and meaningful healing.

Dr. Doll
The Prevention Advocate

✉ info@DrDollConsults.com
🌐 www.DrDollConsults.com
📘 Dr.Doll
📷 Dr.DollConsults
♪ DrDollConsults

- Community Psychologist
- Educator
- Mentor

ANT THE PROPHET

Listen To Atlanta's Rising Musical Visionary

ROCK WITH YOU
ANT THE PROPHET

THAT GIRL
ANT THE PROPHET

YOUNG FLY PROPHET
ANT THE PROPHET X YFN
TRAE POUND

In the epicenter of Atlanta's pulsating music scene, one name has emerged as a beacon of talent and innovation—Ant The Prophet. Teaming up with the accomplished artist YFN Trae Pound, Ant has unleashed the scorching mixtape "Young Fly Prophet," a sonic testament to their combined prowess. This dynamic duo seamlessly blends their unique styles, creating a musical masterpiece that transcends genres and captivates audiences.

But Ant The Prophet's musical journey doesn't stop there. He's set the charts on fire with not one, but two blazing singles—"Rock with You" and "That Girl." These tracks showcase Ant's versatility and knack for crafting catchy tunes that resonate with fans far and wide. "Rock with You" is an infectious melody that's impossible not to groove to, while "That Girl" unveils a more soulful and emotive side of his artistry. Both singles demonstrate Ant's ability to connect with listeners on a deeply personal level, making him a rising star to watch in Atlanta's flourishing music scene.

Ant The Prophet's meteoric rise in Atlanta's music industry is undeniable, and "Young Fly Prophet" along with his hit singles are clear evidence of his talent and potential. With each note and verse, he's carving out a distinct path in the music world, one that promises to lead to even greater heights in the future. As Ant's star continues to ascend, there's no doubt that his name will remain synonymous with innovation, creativity, and the undeniable rhythm of Atlanta.

EGYPTARMANI

EGYPTARMANI: A
MULTIFACETED
CREATIVE FORCE
REDEFINING CHICAGO'S
ARTISTIC LANDSCAPE"

Egyptarmani, a dynamic creative force in the heart of Chicago, is leaving an everlasting stamp on the city's artistic environment. This multidimensional businesswoman has braided her skills as a model, producer, engineer, and vocalist into a tapestry of inspiration and creativity. Her journey exemplifies a never-ending pursuit of artistic greatness and a dedication to pushing limits.

Egyptarmani, as a model, draws attention with her remarkable appearance and ability to bring any idea to life. Her abilities as a producer and engineer lend a new dimension to her creative abilities, as she orchestrates and engineers the sounds that complement her compelling visuals. Her singing ability is the cherry on top, injecting passion and heart into her music. Egyptarmani's exceptional ability to integrate these positions seamlessly distinguishes her, making her a true Chicago entrepreneurial marvel that the rest of the globe is beginning to notice. She is a visionary entrepreneur who is changing the possibilities of creative expression in Chicago and beyond.

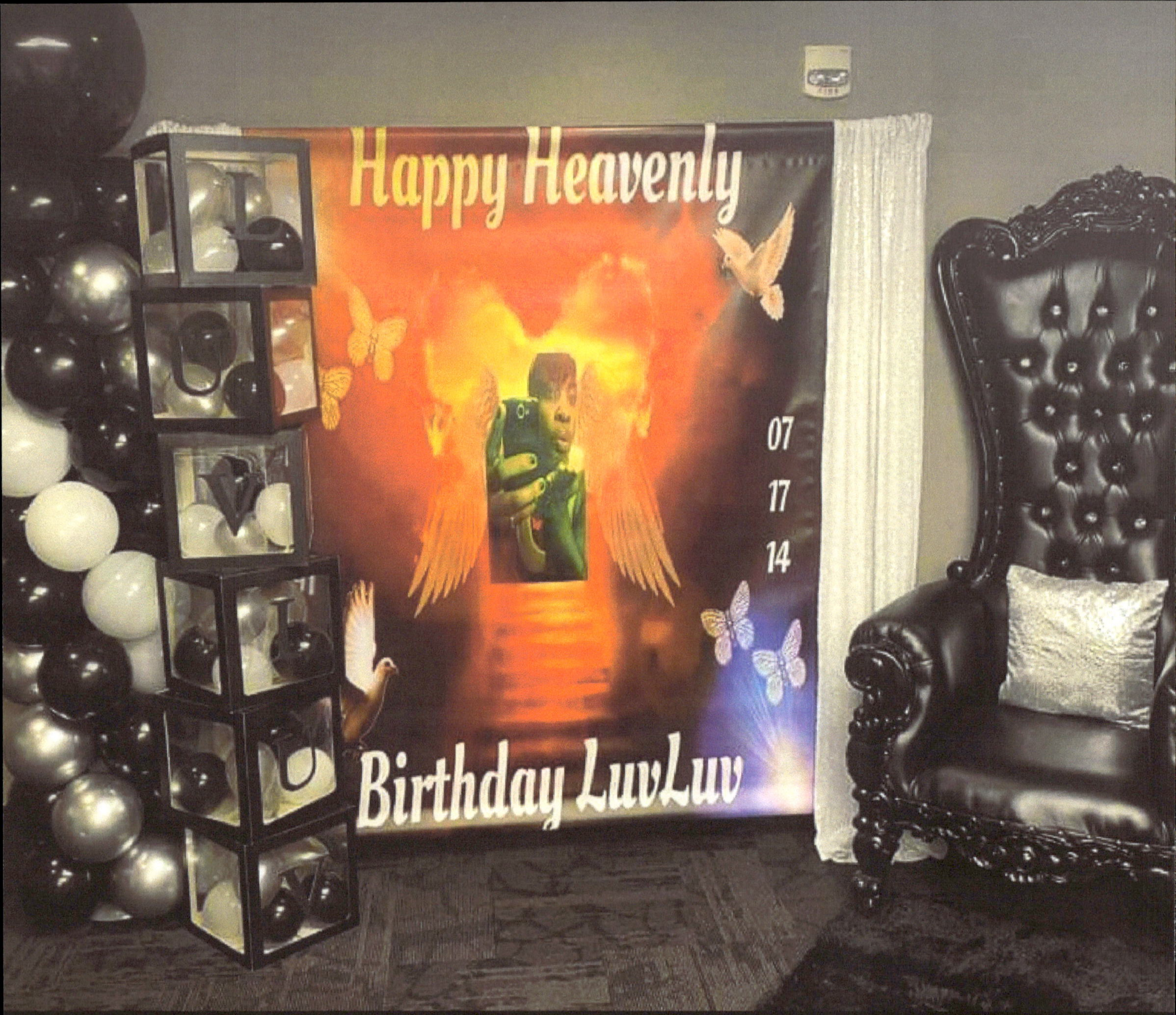

NIQUE'S & NOTTS
CREATIONS

In the bustling heart of Illinois, an event planning dynamo by the name of Dominique is making waves with her extraordinary venture, "Nique's & Notts Creations." Her passion and talent for orchestrating the most magical moments imaginable have elevated her to the status of Illinois' go-to event planner. From the sweetness of baby showers to the grandeur of weddings and everything in between, Nique is the mastermind behind countless unforgettable occasions.

Nique's expertise lies in her ability to transform ordinary gatherings into unforgettable memories. Her baby showers are nothing short of enchanting, with themes that bring parents' dreams to life. From whimsical woodland wonderlands to elegant gender reveals, Nique's & Notts Creations infuses each celebration with creativity and care.

For birthdays, Nique's touch adds a dash of wonder and whimsy that captivates guests of all ages. Whether it's a child's first milestone or a milestone birthday, her eye for detail and penchant for innovative themes make each event a unique and memorable experience.

However, where Nique truly shines is in the realm of weddings. As couples embark on their lifelong journey together, Nique ensures that their special day is an unparalleled reflection of their love story. With meticulous planning and an extensive network of trusted vendors, she crafts weddings that are nothing short of fairy tales.

Nique's & Notts Creations is not just an event planning company; it's an embodiment of creativity, dedication, and personalized service. Nique's unwavering commitment to her clients, combined with her impeccable taste and attention to detail, has made her an indispensable asset to those seeking to turn their dreams into reality.

In a world where every occasion deserves to be celebrated uniquely, Nique's & Notts Creations is the guiding light that turns visions into vivid realities. Whether it's a joyous baby shower, a spectacular birthday bash, or a breathtaking wedding, Nique's touch ensures that every moment is etched in the hearts of those who experience it. Illinois has found its event planning maestro in Nique, and her magical touch is poised to leave a lasting mark on the events landscape for years to come.

Let Me Rant Podcast

By: Kristy Parque

WHO IS KRISTY PARQUE?

I graduated from Valparaiso University in 2019 with a BA in Creative Writing & Cinema Media Studies. While I was at Valpo, I took many courses on filmmaking and script creation. My specialities are videography, lighting, screenwriting, and more. When I was at Valpo , I was a mentor in the S.M.A.R.T Mentoring Program. I mentored incoming students to maintain the retention rate of students of various cultural backgrounds.My tasks were meeting with my mentee every other week to discuss school, to give advice, and to inform them of resources that would be helpful to their success at Valpo. Also, I was a member of BSO and a desk attendant at Beacon Hall.

In 2019, I was an intern at Salem Baptist Church in their Yellow Door Project program. I was a writer and assistant director for their 2019 Christmas play. The Christmas program was televised on WJYS and it was about four stories that highlighted people from different age ranges and how their life experiences brought hope for Christmas. The purpose of the project was to appeal to various age groups with stories that were inspirational and relatable. Some of the responsibilities that I had were writing a scene, being an assistant director, scouting actors, and facilitating rehearsals. Currently I am an academic counselor.
Let me Rant was an idea that I came up with during the Covid 19 shutdown. I was tired of not being able to go anywhere, so I started the podcast to talk about different topics.Let Me Rant is my everything podcast where I interview people from art backgrounds, business owners and people who make significant impacts on the community. I will be launching a video version and short films as well.Also, I have been writing poetry since I was in elementary school. Poetry helps me to weather through the storms of life. I see poetry as soup for the soul.

Poems by Kristy Parque

DESCENDANTS OF MARTYRS
BY K.PARQUE

We are sons, we are daughters, we are the descendants of martyrs we are still in slavery cause never departed, our minds are still in chains, but our hearts are not in bondage, we must break free from society's limits on us, but can't nobody stop us but us. The Black Panther Party said power to the people even though we were in a society where we continuously face evil. We were born with societies stain so we must stop and honor the slain and make the world know our names.

We must stand together divided we fall but united we stand tall. We were once so blind. Now we can see clear we hit the glass ceiling, but the sunshine is near, a moment of glory that seems to disappear.

Yeah, I know you cry at night you walk these streets scared. In the end, you will fly high because in life to succeed you will have to fight, in the end you will eventually get it right. Your pain is your story, your life reflects your glory. You were going to give up, but you saw a bright future then you looked up.

No more rainy days or skies full of gray time to stop putting your life on replay fast forward because you will see better days. You dream big but you act hard. You're afraid to tell people who you really are, but you were born to be great, born to be a star, no time to wait your future is not that far.

In the end you'll soar like an eagle; its power in your words is destined for the people. We strain for survival in a world filled with evil; the time is now time to free the people.

Unforgettable by K. Parque
(in Memory of my Granny)

Live your life to the fullest is the mantra. I'm just trying to be an influence like Frank Sinatra. I have an old soul like Nat King Cole. I want to break the mold to adjust how a story is told.

You see you are unforgettable. You made me who I am & that's a fact for many years you got me on track. You were a fighter, the true definition of a bounce back. You always focused on what I had instead of what I lacked, & you told me the truth that was that.

You inspired me & started a fire in me that made me feel reborn. You were a pleasant presence in the time of storm.
We used to talk 5 times a day, the moments never passed away. You taught me to pray about everything. You told me that when I felt that no one was listening to stand tall, lift my voice, & sing.

You taught me the value of being life smart not just book smart. You taught me to finish what I start. You believed in me & gave me my wings.
Now I can fly & every time I look to the sky...I see you, I miss you, because you are unforgettable.

Dirty Wounds
by K.Parque

Blood falls from the sky instead of rain and it splashes continuously on my windowpane.
It injects like a needle and leaves a stain, God, please come to erase my pain.
The past is not what I gain the future seems like nothing but rain.
Together it won't be such a strain. Our strength and determination are what keep us sane.
Who is to blame? The past continues to baffle my brain, but the future continuously calls my name.
They say clean your wounds, so they don't get infected,
but the truth is they prevent old dreams and nightmares from being resurrected.
Some memories are better if they are not recollected.
These wounds are like puzzle pieces, without the missing piece, it can't be connected.
Dirty wounds that are a signal to wounds that come from deep inside.
You will forever be named strong , with a spirit and soul that will never die.

Why did I write this?

I wrote this poem to talk about the importance of knowing who you are and continuing to fight for what you believe in. I am very open-minded, and it is essential to speak up for yourself and others that are facing injustice. I wrote this power to help people to feel empowered to push on no matter what.

No one is perfect but everyone is a work in progress. It is important to never be silenced despite whatever life throws at you. Know that tomorrow will be better than yesterday, but you must be courageous to see the changes that you desire. Do not be afraid of change.

Where you are from does not have to determine where you are going. Each time period in your life helps you to build you to realize your purpose.

Why did I write this?

I wrote this to help myself to cope with the death of my granny. My granny was one of my best friends and she was supportive of me. She would attend my school events from elementary school to undergrad. She invested in my education as well and was very present in my life.

In life we all may lose someone that is important to us, but we must continue their legacy to honor them with our words and actions. It is important to be able to cope with the loss of a loved one. Sometimes you might not know who to turn to or how to cope but using your gifts and talents can be beneficial.

It is essential to focus on the beautiful memories of your loved one to help you through your grieving period. Use that grief as motivation to excel in everything that you do to make them proud. Appreciate the living and cherish the dead.

Why did I write this?

In life we all go through pain and sometimes it leaves us feeling wounded. We have two choices to give those wounds the time to heal or to let them eat us alive. I use wounds in a literal & symbolic way because sometimes we all have emotional wounds then can turn into physical wounds/ailments. It is important to make sure that we focus on the positive things in life. Do not allow your past pain and experiences to break you. Do not let the dirt(which represents life issues) prevent your emotional wounds from healing.

You are not your past you are stronger because of it. Always know that no matter what you are going through you are not in this world alone. There is someone somewhere out there that loves you.

Going through pain might make you feel wounded and down, but it will not destroy you. Use every life experience as a building block to get through it because you will emerge stronger after the storm.

"POETRY IS LIKE SOUP FOR YOUR SOUL".
- KRISTY PARQUE "LET ME RANT PODCAST"
NEW PODCAST EPISODES WILL BE RELEASED EVERY FRIDAY AT 7PM STARTING NOVEMBER 17TH.
IG:QUEENARI_97
KPARQUE42@GMAIL.COM

MADAME LUCYY

Listen To Chicago's Hip-Hop Crown Jewel

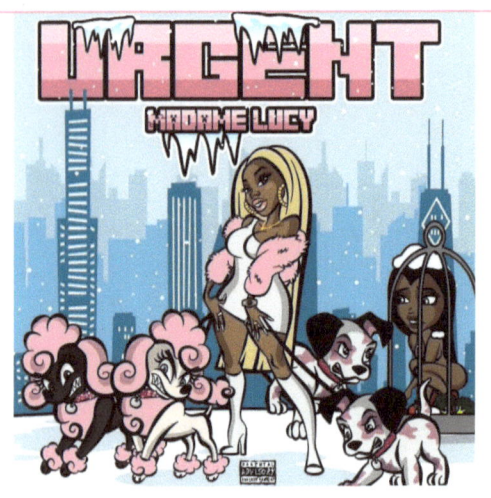

URGENT
MADAME LUCYY

SCARFACE
MADAME LUCYY

BLING BLING
MADAME LUCYY

16

RAPPER, LYRICIST, PHILANTHROPIST, AND EXTRAORDINARY ENTREPRENEUR MADAME LUCYY IS REDEFINING THE CREATIVE SCENERY OF CHICAGO.

A dynamic entrepreneur has taken center stage in Chicago, pushing the boundaries of innovation, community participation, and business savvy. Meet Madame Lucyy, an artist, composer, volunteer, and networking powerhouse who exemplifies the spirit of inventiveness and compassion.

Madame Lucyy's amazing talent as a rapper has brought the dynamic energy of Chicago's music culture to life. Her songs ring true with genuine sincerity and lyrical genius, cementing her place in the city's hip-hop culture. Her catchy tunes not only capture the essence of city life, but also provide an empowering narrative that connects with her audience.

She is a community builder as well as an artist. Her dedication to volunteer work and community service is reflected in the good impact she has had on the lives of those around her. Whether she's participating in community activities, mentoring budding talents, or supporting philanthropic organizations, she applies her passion and drive to uplift her community, demonstrating that success is about more than just personal gain.

Madame Lucyy's business acumen extends to her network. She works frequently with other entrepreneurs, sharing ideas and experience to encourage business innovation. Her ability to connect and encourage like-minded individuals has resulted in a thriving creative and entrepreneurial ecosystem in Chicago.

She exemplifies how an artist, singer, volunteer, and entrepreneur can smoothly combine their talents, values, and ambitions to have a lasting influence on their community. Her journey exemplifies a beautiful blend of art, business, and social responsibility, demonstrating that true success transcends individual ambitions and is about making a significant and lasting contribution to the world. Madame Lucyy's imprint on Chicago's creative and entrepreneurial scene is expanding, indicating that exciting changes are on the way.

ADVERTISEMENT HERE

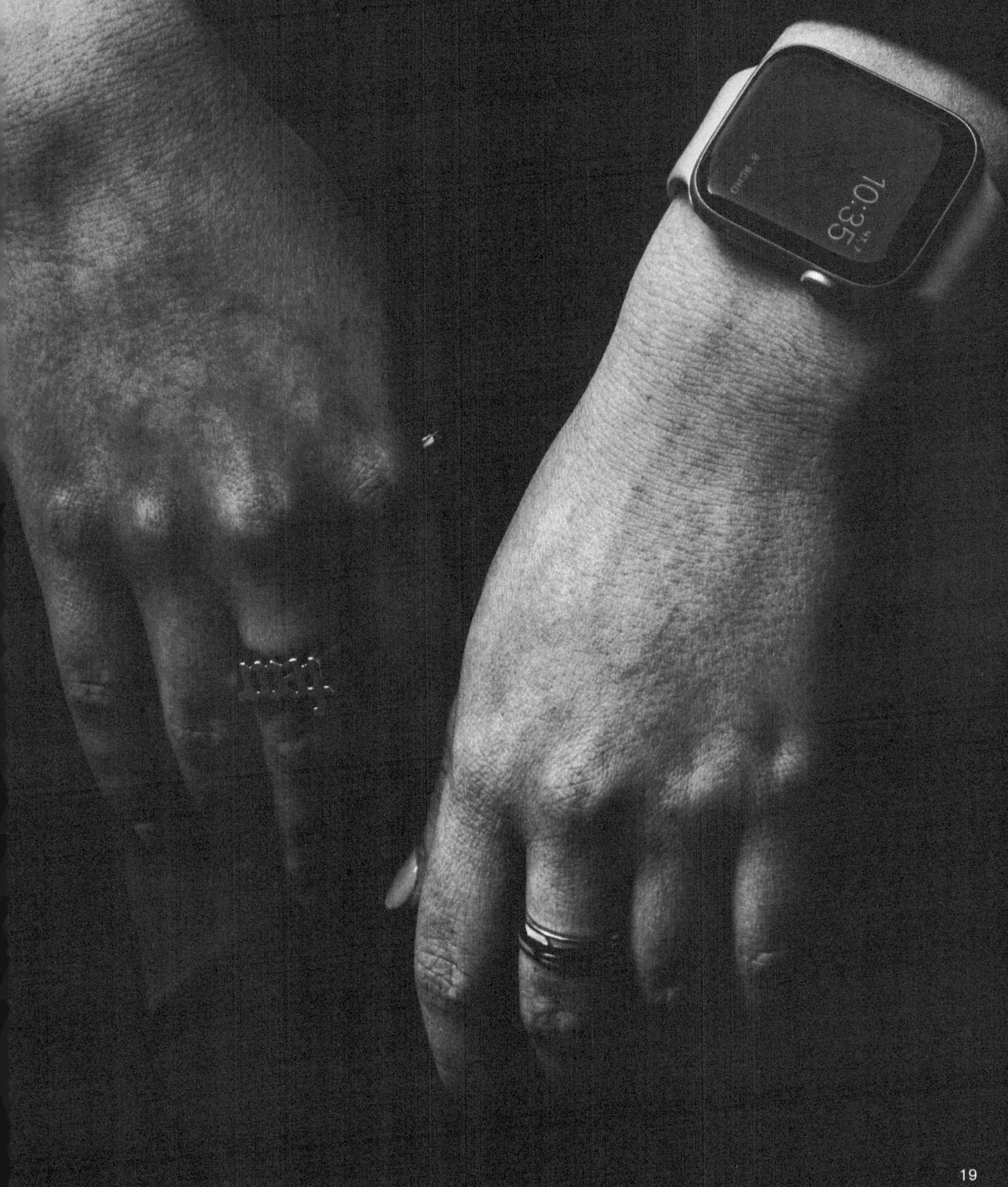

19

ADVERTISE WITH SLNP UNSIGNED

SLNP UNSIGNED

GALLERY

10/24
ISSUE 02